# Government Actuary's Department
# Spring 2006 Departmental Report

## The Government's Expenditure Plans
## 2006-07 to 2007-08

*Presented to Parliament by the Economic Secretary to the Treasury and the Chief Secretary to the Treasury by Command of Her Majesty May 2006*



Cm 6831

£7.50

## Contents Page

## A message from the Government Actuary

The year 2005-06 saw GAD in a strong financial position and experiencing an unprecedented level of demand for our services. We are actively recruiting to build up our technical resources to keep pace with the demand. One of the major factors in this has been the Public Service Forum discussions on the future of the main public service pension schemes. Not only has there been a huge amount of central activity on developing the policy for the public services as a whole, but also intensive discussions about possible reforms to each of the major pension schemes that we advise.

For funded schemes there have been many new challenges, as the provisions of the Pensions Act 2004 come into force, with scheme-specific funding requirements, decisions on prudent technical provisions to be taken by trustees rather than the Scheme Actuary, matters for the trustees to negotiate with the employers, considerations relating to the Pension Protection Fund levy and many more.

GAD also participated in some high profile activity on the pension policy front, with advice on a great many current topics to the Department for Work and Pensions (DWP), the Pension Protection Fund and the Pensions Regulator. We also carried out a quinquennial review of the contracted-out rebate, beginning with a public consultation and leading up to a report to Parliament and a recommendation for the rebate level for 2007-12.

Last year saw the implementation of some key Morris Review recommendations. From February 2006 responsibility for the national population projections and life tables was transferred to the National Statistics Centre for Demography (NSCD), a newly formed division of the Office for National Statistics (ONS). GAD will, however, continue to provide advice to NSCD on mortality matters. The 2004-based set of population projections were published in October 2005, to a very challenging timetable, with a range of variant projections published with the principal projections for the first time.

We have also said goodbye to several staff who have transferred to DWP and to HM Revenue & Customs (HMRC), with a view to performing more of the day-to-day modelling and analysis work for the UK social security scheme within those two departments. GAD will still be responsible for the formal reports to Parliament on the National Insurance Fund (NIF), so we have retained the capability to perform that role, as well as to be able to continue to provide advice to many social security schemes in other jurisdictions.

GAD published the 2004 Occupational Pensions Scheme Survey in very timely fashion in mid-2005, having had a particularly good response rate this time from pension administrators. Work is already well underway towards the publication of the 2005 survey in June 2006, although, in line with the Morris Review recommendation, it is likely that responsibility for the survey will thereafter pass to the Office for National Statistics.

To make the most efficient use of space, and to strengthen our finances so as to limit the need for increases in our fee rates, we consolidated our accommodation from four to three floors of Finlaison House, enabling us to let out space to other public bodies on the ground floor as well as the top two floors.

GAD is a pre-eminent source of actuarial advice and guidance for departments and public sector bodies, as our experts combine the professional skills required by our clients with a commitment to public service. GAD is able to advise Ministers and public sector clients with professional independence and without the same commercial conflicts that private firms have.

The development in 2005 of a new pension valuation system, working in cooperation with our software supplier, has given us a strong platform to continue to deliver the best quality pensions advice and support for our clients. This will continue to be developed over the next few months and our clients will reap the benefits of improved efficiency and greater flexibility. We continue to offer best quality service, tailored to the needs of the public sector, and this is well recognised by most of our clients.

So what can we expect in 2006-07 and how will the Department continue to meet the demands of clients in the short and medium term? We will continue to invest in new systems and to improve the efficiency of our working processes. We will focus our expertise in particular areas into specialist teams who can leverage the necessary skill sets. We will be more proactive in marketing our services, so as to build up our position in what is expected to become an increasingly competitive marketplace.

**Chris Daykin**

Government Actuary

**May 2006**

## About the Government Actuary's Department

### *Our history*

The Government Actuary's Department (GAD) has functioned as a separate department since 1919. It was created to provide actuarial services to Ministers and Government departments. Although our range of activities has broadened considerably since those early days, our primary purpose has remained unchanged.

### *Our Aims and Objectives*

The Government Actuary's Department's (GAD's) fundamental aim is:

> *To provide mainly public sector clients with independent, professional, actuarial advice of the highest quality.*

Our main objectives are:

- To offer high quality client-orientated service to clients at all times.
- To maintain the highest standards of professionalism and relevance in the giving of actuarial advice.
- To provide clients with value for money in the provision of actuarial services.
- To maintain a well-trained and well-motivated staff with up-to-date skills and expertise.

Meeting these aims and objectives is the responsibility of the Government Actuary, supported by the Management Board and his senior management team. He is answerable to the Economic Secretary to the Treasury who has ministerial responsibility for the department.

Our minister and clients together are our principal stakeholders.

### *What makes us different from a private sector actuarial firm*

For our public sector clients in particular we exist to:

- offer independent actuarial advice, free from commercial pressures;
- offer confidentiality on sensitive political or commercial issues;
- deliver consistent advice across the public sector – this is particularly important for the public service pension schemes;
- offer value for money to our customers in the fee structure we use; and
- provide a cost-effective government actuarial service with a strong professional ethos.

We believe clients choose us because we

- are not driven by a profit motive;
- have no conflict created by the interests of private sector clients;
- are part of the public service, so we understand the constraints and the considerations which affect decision-making in that environment; and
- give advice that is not influenced by a wish to sell other services.

It has always been important for us to be seen as a provider of good value, high quality actuarial services to government and public sector bodies around the world.

***Our Expertise***

There are a number of main branches of actuarial practice in the UK but each of these relies on the assessment, analysis and management of different types of risk, primarily financial risk. The main branches of our expertise are:

- Pensions
- Social Insurance
- Life Insurance
- General Insurance
- Investment
- Health Care

We can also provide assistance with modelling for manpower planning and with other employee benefits, including redundancy packages.

With our public service focus, GAD's main areas of activity in the UK are pensions and social insurance. Internationally, the main activities are social insurance, pension reform and pension and insurance regulation. GAD is also advising on the financing of health care, risk management and strategic investment and asset/liability considerations.

Demand for our services is higher than ever and we are recruiting additional actuaries, actuarial trainees and other numerate graduates to help us meet the demands of our clients. Further developments in systems and processes will help us deliver an even more efficient service to our clients.

***Our financial structure***

For most of the twentieth century GAD was voted monies by Parliament to provide the advice which other parts of government required. The move towards greater transparency of costs across the public services led, in April 1989, to a full repayment régime being introduced for GAD. All those who commission us to advise them, from the public or private sector, from the UK or overseas, are required to pay fees for the services they receive. Those charges must cover the full cost of that advice.

GAD has retained a small net Parliamentary vote (around 10% of overall expenditure) to deliver "core" activities (principally the national population projections and life tables and the annual Occupational Pension Scheme Survey), which could not be attributed to a single owner. The Morris Review, the recommendations of which were accepted by HM Treasury in March 2005, required GAD to transfer most of these activities elsewhere within government with the consequent loss of most of our net voted funds.

These changes mean that our resource funding now has to be almost entirely found from the fees we charge to our clients. However, GAD remains confident that the loss of most of the Vote funding will not significantly impact on its ability to operate. GAD is actively expanding both its UK pensions advice and its international activities. We have confidence that GAD has priced its services competitively and continues to offer services that our clients recognise and value.

***Our operational structure and risk management***

We have a streamlined management and operation structure in keeping with our size and being flexible and dynamic as a service provider. We are organised into UK and overseas business and central services. The Government Actuary is accountable for the running of the department. He is supported by the Management Board, which he chairs. The Board has two non-executive directors from the private sector and four senior managers for the business areas. Responsibility for day-to-day running rests with the Operations Committee chaired by the Deputy Government Actuary (and head of UK Business) with the head of international business, the Director of Finance and the Personnel Director.

Other working groups and committees report to the Board on specific aspects of professional work and operations.

A risk assessment group advises the Operations Committee on risk management which in turn assigns risks to individual managers as well as monitoring and reviewing risks and their control. Risk management is regularly reviewed by the Audit Committee and Internal Auditor.

More information is given in Annex A.

***Our people***

The success of GAD is critically dependent on having staff who perform to the highest standards. This applies across the department: to those who are working with clients, those who are managing our operations and those who are providing infrastructure and support on which others depend. Our programme of selection, training and development is aimed at ensuring that everyone can gain the skills and experience to realise their full potential. For such a small organisation we have a very wide range of personal attributes, a diversity which we treasure.

Our qualified actuaries are, for example, drawn from a wide range of backgrounds, many of them having worked in the private sector before joining GAD, as well as a good number we have recruited as graduates and developed within the department.

The actuarial profession is comparatively small. It is important for the public service and for a healthy profession that GAD plays its part in training the actuaries of the future in the needs of the public service and that we encourage all our actuarial staff to be active in the many committees and working parties on which the profession depends.

## The Work We Do

### *The overall structure of the department*

The organisation is split into two main business areas: UK Business (Public Sector Pensions and Pensions Policy) and International Business (Pension Reform, Regulation of Insurance and Pensions and Social Insurance (this last also for the UK)). These are supported by the Corporate Centre (Central Services).

### *The Work of the Actuarial Business Teams*

Although we work for a wide range of clients, there is a significant group for whom we provide continuing service each year. We expect these to form the major part of our business for the lifetime of these spending plans. Each team has, however, set its own targets for service delivery as shown below.

*UK Business*

The UK Business teams will provide actuarial support on demand to a wide range of clients, whether pension schemes, employers or other scheme sponsors. A significant activity is advising contracting authorities on the implications of the Fair Deal policy on staff transfers, both within and across the boundary of the public service, and assessing proposals from potential contractors for meeting the broad comparability standard and other aspects of staff transfers. Other major areas of activity include:

- Ongoing and wide-ranging actuarial and pension consultancy advice to public sector, near public sector and private sector pension schemes, both funded and unfunded, including for a number of schemes, Scheme Actuary responsibilities under the Pensions Act 2004. For example, we advise on benefit design and cost, financing and investment strategy.
- Advice to government departments, including HM Treasury, on policy for pension provision within the public sector, taxation considerations relating to pensions, specific individual pensions issues and supervisory matters.
- Advising on accounting for pensions liabilities and preparing appropriate disclosures of funded and unfunded pension liabilities.
- Working to ensure that government policy protecting employees' pension rights on transfers from public sector pension schemes is implemented on behalf of sponsoring departments and public sector employers, and that the interests of the taxpayer are protected in Public Private Partnerships (PPP), Private Finance Initiative (PFI) and other reorganisation exercises and machinery of government changes.
- Other ad-hoc jobs, including compensation assessments, appearing as expert witnesses arbitration work, second opinions and wider financing and design issues for pension schemes in the UK.
- Social Security and Pensions policy – advising DWP and HM Revenue & Customs on policy for social security and all aspects of occupational, personal and stakeholder pensions.

- Advising the DWP and HM Treasury on the terms for contracting out of the State Second Pension;
- Occupational Pension Scheme Survey 2005 – we designed the questionnaire and the sample, and analysed the results and will publish the final report of this authoritative review on our website in June 2006.
- Assessment of damages and loss of pension rights – advice to the Courts and Tribunals on how to set a value on future financial loss.
- Health and long-term care – advice on long-term financing issues for health and long-term care.
- Miscellaneous items – including verification of the statistical randomness of the Premium Bond system.
- Providing advice to the Pensions Regulator (tPR), including having two actuaries seconded full-time in the Brighton office, and to the Pension Protection Fund (PPF).

These activities and the work for other clients (wider public sector and overseas schemes) are shared amongst these teams.

*International Business*

The International Business team predominantly supports work on Social Insurance and on Insurance Regulation and Supervision, including:

- Social Security schemes – undertaking statutory duties in advising on the finances of the National Insurance Fund (GB);
- Advising overseas governments on the design and financing of social security schemes;
- Advising the DWP and HM Revenue & Customs on the financial aspects of the National Insurance benefits and contributions;
- Supervision of Insurance – advising on the regulation of the insurance industry and on the supervision of individual insurance companies in a number of jurisdictions outside the UK.

*All teams*

Regardless of client, both actuarial business units must ensure that GAD:

- organises itself so as to be able to give a good quality of service to Ministers and other government departments at all times and does not diversify activities to an extent which would compromise this service delivery;
- diversifies its client base, particularly within the broad public sector in the UK and overseas to ensure a cost-effective staffing and fee structure and adequate breadth of expertise;
- maintains practical experience of advising a reasonable number of funded pension clients including those which are subject to the full requirements of the Pensions Act 2004;

- actively promotes its services at home and abroad to all parts of government and the public sector;
- always seeks to obtain a satisfactory level of remuneration for work undertaken, except where
  - it is deemed to be in the public interest to act or to undertake work for which it is not clear that the effort will be directly or fully reimbursed; or
  - the work may provide valuable spin-offs in terms, for example, of training and development opportunities, information gathering or potential new business.

*Dealing with the public*

GAD is happy to be contacted by members of the public on any of its activities. We maintain a website which provides a range of information on GAD and its work, as well as contact details for phone, post and e-mail. GAD's direct dealings with members of the public are limited. It is our policy that any such contact, including those arising under the Freedom of Information Act, should be dealt with promptly, clearly and helpfully.

## The Efficiency Review

Together with the other Chancellor's Departments, GAD was asked to make efficiency savings to reflect a reducing dependence on vote funding. At the time the department offered savings of 11% of our then resource vote (some £120k) to be found in the three years 2005-08. We were delighted to achieve these savings in full in 2005-06. A significant saving initiative, which was later agreed, was to sublet one of our floors.

Below are the key areas where the department has made significant efficiency savings in 2005-06:

- GAD has freed up all its actuarial and fee earning staff to concentrate solely on client chargeable work by strengthening its client liaison and research sections with staff from the support functions. Together with an increase in client demand, this has resulted in our fee-earning staff achieving a significant increase in productivity (chargeable hours sold). Figures for 2005-06 show an efficiency saving of around £600K, which will be confirmed when our accounts are prepared.
- GAD has sublet one floor of the building to another government client (The Human Tissue Authority). This required a re-location of some 20% of personnel to other floors already occupied by GAD. The rental saving achieved in 2005-06 was £117K.
- The new sub-letting arrangement (we already let two floors) has in additional yielded savings on facility management and council tax charges. The saving in 2005-06 was £108K
- The new sub-tenant has also agreed to buy corporate services from GAD. A Service Level Agreement is now in place for the following services which generated £67K in 2005-06:

    1. IT Support Services
    2. Internal Audit services
    3. Financial services – all transaction services
    4. Strategic and Business finance service

## Our strategies and finances in more detail

GAD works hard to ensure compliance with all Central Government initiatives, although the small size of the department means that this can be a challenge, especially as GAD also has to operate as a competitive business and generate fee income to recover costs in full. We continually strive to cut our costs and to make our services more efficient, whilst retaining an important emphasis on the quality of advice given, thus providing good value for money to all our clients.

Apart from setting targets for our actuarial business units, we also set strategies for the support teams, who play an essential role in the delivery of our actuarial services through the support they provide. Annexes B to F set out the main elements of the strategies in the support areas and Annex G considers how we are faring relative to our Performance Management Indicators. Annex H sets out the core tables on financing, showing past history and projections for the future.

## Management structure

The head of UK business (Deputy Government Actuary), the head of overseas business (Chief Actuary), Director of Finance (Grade 7) and Director of Personnel (Grade 7) report to the Government Actuary, who is the Head of Department and Accounting Officer. There are four business units within the UK, two covering public service pensions, one for wider public sector pensions and one for pension policy. Each of these units is headed by a Chief Actuary. The Director of Personnel is responsible for human resources, information technology and office services.

GAD is not formally covered by the senior civil service. A number of posts have equivalent job weight to those in the SCS.

| | Number | Pay band (£000s) |
|---|---|---|
| Government Actuary | 1 | 142-200 |
| Deputy Government Actuary | 1 | 111-143 |
| Chief Actuaries | 5 | 93-126 |

### GAD committee structure

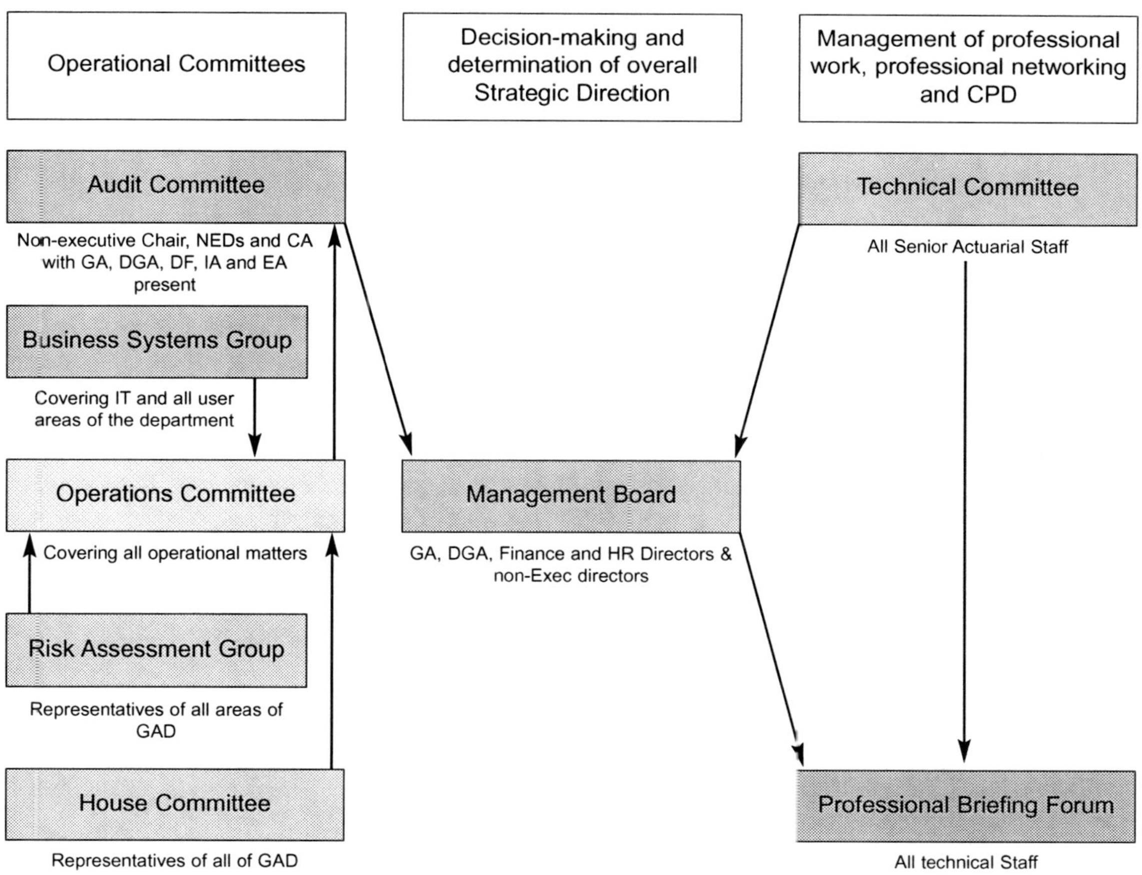


**Board and Committees within the Government Actuary's Department**

# Human Resources Strategy

### *Retaining and Recruiting Staff*

GAD needs to recruit and retain staff at sufficient levels to provide services to meet client needs. As a net régime, the costs of additional staff are fully covered by the income achieved. Our strategy for staffing is, therefore, as noted below –

- recruit and train an adequate number of staff with recognized actuarial qualifications, or as trainees prepared to study with a view to obtaining such qualifications;
- maintain our professional staff with up-to-date knowledge of relevant actuarial and related topics through Continuing Professional Development;
- maintain sufficient professional staff satisfying specific practising requirements set by the UK actuarial profession, for example to act as Scheme Actuaries to pension fund clients;
- provide sufficient variety and depth of client work to train professional staff and to give them a grounding in the operation and financial management of pension funds, social security schemes and insurance companies (for our overseas market), particularly with a view to the need to maintain an adequate capability to advise Ministers and departments on the relevant policy issues;
- recruit and retain an adequate number of technical, administrative, executive and other staff to perform all the necessary support functions and to assist actuarial staff in areas where it is appropriate and cost-effective for work to be done by non-actuaries;
- motivate and reward staff according to competencies, responsibility and performance, having regard to the need for fairness, openness, market salary levels and the overriding need to staff the Department at a level which will enable the objectives to be fulfilled;
- negotiate pay and grading arrangements for all members of staff;
- maintain the capacity to carry out relevant research and to ensure that GAD can sustain a high standard of technical advice in line with the types of service provided by private sector consulting firms;
- monitor the quality and timeliness of advice to clients and ensure that the service is provided in as efficient and cost-effective a way as possible.

## Training and Development Strategy

GAD is an accredited Investor in People and is committed to giving all its staff the opportunity to develop their skills and potential in support of GAD business.

GAD has a substantial budget for training to allow for training programmes and professional actuarial examinations, together with training for other professions represented in the department. In addition, the department provides general computer and Management Development training for all members of staff. Each annual performance round involves consideration of the required training to develop an individual; this training needs requirement is fed into an annual training plan for the department. The development of all our staff is of paramount importance to the management team of GAD.

Scheme actuaries of funded UK pension schemes are required, under mandatory rules laid down by the UK Actuarial Profession, to fulfil annually the requirements of the Continuing Professional Development (CPD) Scheme in order to have their practising certificates renewed. The Government Actuary and a number of the qualified actuaries in the UK Business area have Scheme Actuary practising certificates and are affected directly by this requirement. The CPD Scheme requires a minimum of 15 hours verifiable CPD per year, 10 hours of which must be directly relevant to the subject matter of the practising certificate and at least 5 hours of which must come from activities that are external to GAD.

During the coming year, mandatory CPD requirements will be extended to all working actuaries in the UK, although the rules will be somewhat less strict for those not requiring a practising certificate. All actuaries should spend at least two hours a year on skills relevant to their work but outside the technical specialism. This should include some training in professionalism and ethics. GAD is committed to providing the resources to enable all qualified actuaries in the department to complete the recommended amount of CPD.

Non-actuarial staff are encouraged to pursue their personal development by studying for additional qualifications. We currently sponsor training programmes for members of staff in professional accountancy training (CIMA and ACCA), training towards graduate membership of the Chartered Institute of Personnel and Development (CIPD), professional pensions training (PMI), statistical, computer science qualifications (like MCSE) and Health and Safety qualifications. As with other government departments, we also encourage personal development through degree studies (members of GAD are currently studying with a small amount of study leave granted per year with Birkbeck University and Open University – most of the studies are undertaken in their spare time).

In the next few years we will need to provide training for marketing skills together with customer service qualifications. These will all be used as part of our on-going plan for improving customer liaison and engaging in more proactive marketing. In addition to professional training, we need to develop skills-based competencies for our support staff (both in the business areas and the corporate centre). Changes to processes and systems over the next three years will require skills, which we will need to develop in-house.

## IT Strategy

New systems and processes have always been important to GAD's delivery of its services to clients. This year will see more development of our existing systems to ensure that we continue to deliver best value for money. Plans for Business Continuity to be embedded off-site, further development of remote working facilities and our existing Virtual Private Network (VPN) will allow us to respond more flexibly to the needs of our staff and to ensure minimum system downtime in the future.

### *Management Information System (MIS)*

The system continues to support effective financial reporting for the Management Board and further enhancements to system will support the goal of the Department to achieve a pre-summer recess timetable for the completion of Resource Accounts. Looking forward we will be developing facilities for reporting to project managers from the information collected.

### *Electronic Records Management (ERMS)*

In 2005-06 we piloted an Electronic Records Management System. Results from that trial were not promising. We are investigating other options for improving records and document management in a digital format.

### *Business Continuity Planning*

To further balance the requirement for continuous available service, GAD is developing the details of a business continuity plan. Major components are already in place with the acquisition of an offsite back-up servers and provision of accommodation for key staff outside of the building.

### *Pensions Valuation Software*

Further developments, enhancements and improvements to the pension valuations software will be made in 2006-07. All these improvements will assist in enhancing our capability as well as delivering value for money and better service for clients.

### *Extending our business links*

Effective and secure electronic communications with our clients is ever more important. After a long wait, a small systems GSI solution has now been released and GAD is in the process of adaptation.

# Office Services Strategy

## Accommodation strategy

GAD continues to operate on two floors of the building with a floor of meeting rooms. The other three floors of the building are leased to sub-tenants, who also share the costs of facilities management for the building.

### *Paper filing*

We will continue to rely on paper storage for a significant number of years. We have practical plans to ensure that future materials will be stored electronically and are investigating tools to improve record retrieval.

### *Library and Information Services*

GAD is very proud of both its library services and the ability of our information management staff to research on behalf of our clients and colleagues alike. We have links to library resources outside the department and share materials with the UK Actuarial Profession's library.

### *Shared Services*

In line with government best practice we are pleased to offer shared services for accommodation, IT, Finance, Internal Audit and other office services to our sub-tenants.

### *Enhancements to building facilities*

We took the opportunity at the end of 2005-06 to improve facilities in the building for the benefit of all tenants. Specifically, we are introducing more up-to-date security systems, Personal Announcement system and a Deaf Alerter system on the Lower Ground floor archive room.

## Client Liaison and Marketing Strategy

GAD is pleased to have managed to put more effort into client liaison in the past year. Satisfied clients are essential to the future viability of the Department and we must continue to do as much as possible to give them the service they need.

We have re-affirmed our view that we must:

- offer actuarial advice of the highest quality
- offer a quality service, in terms of timeliness and presentation
- think ahead and identify needs which clients may have in the future
- offer the highest standards of customer service at all times
- carry out work efficiently and offering value for money for clients
- listen to our clients, improve our service and get invoicing right.

GAD must remain totally committed to meeting the requirements of clients and to ensuring their complete and continuing satisfaction with our work. All staff, in every part of GAD, need to be fully aware that the focus of our activities must be, not just on the work itself, but on the way in which that work and output is targeted to meet the needs of our clients. This must include arrangements for appointment, responsiveness to client contacts and demands, availability when clients call, monitoring of tasks in progress, clear and prompt invoicing and the quality of the work product itself.

Client focus requires good communication about client issues and their requirements. It also requires consistent handling of client problems. Appropriate training on client service and satisfaction issues is now part of our Management Development Programme.

### *Marketing*

We have a core of business, which we need to continue to deliver and improve upon both in terms of speed of delivery and value for money. We also wish to discuss with our clients any opportunities for new areas of work in which GAD may be involved. We are able to develop the services we offer and to seek out new clients. We need to do this proactively for several very good reasons:

- to ensure we are providing clients with the service they require
- defensively, to protect ourselves from the risk to the stability of our business
- to expand our fee base in order to reduce the impact of overhead costs
- to maximise the utilisation of our skill base
- to give staff the opportunity to expand their skills and competences.

There may be significant scope for cross-selling, for example in countries where GAD already has credibility in one area. A particular area, which seems ideally suited to the deployment of our skills is work on pension arrangements for public sector employees in other countries. As with growth in other areas, it is important not to overstretch our resources or to undermine our ability to provide good service to key UK clients such as the DWP, MoD, the Treasury and the main public sector pension schemes.

## PMI Targets

### *Departmental Targets*

Like other government departments, GAD agreed Performance Management Indicators (PMIs) under Spending Review 2004 with HM Treasury.

| PMI Targets set under SR 2004 | | Our Achievements against the Targets | | |
|---|---|---|---|---|
| | | At March 2004 | By March 2006 | By March 2007 |
| **Objective 1** – Provide actuarial advice to Government Departments and other GAD clients in respect of employer-sponsored pension arrangements (particularly the main public service pension schemes) and other employee benefits; | | | | |
| **PMI 1** | To maintain our existing Central Government (CG) client base and grow the number of large CG projects by 3% over the next three years. | Our benchmark was 59 UK Government projects large enough to bring in income of £10,000 or more in year. | We have 62 UK Government projects matching this criterion. | We would expect to have at least 65 UK Government projects in place by this date. |
| **PMI 2** | To increase our client base in the wider public sector by an additional 5 clients in the next three years. | Currently we have 93 Wider Public Sector active clients on our books. | This has grown so that we now have 113 Wider Public Sector active clients. | We would expect to have at least 115 Wider Public Sector clients at this time. |
| **Objective 2** – Provide the social security projections, demographic analyses and actuarial advice necessary to underpin Ministerial decision-making in social security and pension policy and to provide the actuarial advice necessary for the regulation and supervision of financial institutions overseas. | | | | |
| **PMI 3** | To maintain the volume of work on overseas contracts involving our Insurance Team over the next three years. | The current annual income is £410k. The fee income should grow to match increases in fees. | The annual income for insurance supervision in 2005-06 was £954k. | With larger contracts being awarded to our insurance team we expect income to be at least £1m. |
| **PMI 4** | To continue to advise UK pensions regulators and pension policy setters with the retention of our advisory role to DWP, HMT and Opra (and its successor body). | GAD holds these contracts. | GAD has retained these contracts and additionally advises the Pension Protection Fund. | GAD will continue to advise all these policy setters. |

| PMI Targets set under SR 2004 | | Our Achievements against the Targets | | |
|---|---|---|---|---|
| | | At March 2004 | By March 2006 | By March 2007 |
| **General Objective – set in our Business Strategy** – *To provide mainly public sector clients with independent, professional, actuarial advice of the highest quality.* | | | | |
| **PMI 5** | To retain high professional standards – to implement a new system of internal peer review with the objective of attaining and maintaining an average rating of 90% or more in peer review assessments on completed major projects each quarter. | Our peer review average rating is currently 90%. | Peer review is carried out for all major projects and assessments confirm that we continue to maintain a very high quality rating on all reports issuing from the department. | Over the next year we intend to formalise further our processes for carrying out peer review on all advice issuing from the department and maintaining a suitably documented audit trail. |
| **PMI 6**<br><br>will | To manage our finances within targets agreed in the Spending Review and to<br><br>publish our Annual Report (including Resource Accounts) within the 'faster closing' timetable set by HM Treasury. | Resource accounts were published in November 2004 –<br><br>within the timetable agreed by HMT. All targets achieved. | Resource accounts for 2005-06 show that we<br><br>managed our finances within the agreed targets. They were presented for audit within the timetable agreed with NAO, with a view to publication of the Annual Report and Accounts before the end | Resource accounts (within voted limits)<br><br>be published by July 2007. |

## Core Data Tables

**Table 1: Government Actuary's Department public spending (£000)**

| | 2000-01 Outturn | 2001-02 Outturn | 2002-03 Outturn | 2003-04 Outturn | 2004-05 Outturn | 2005-06 Estimated Outturn | 2006-07 Plans | 2007-08 Plans |
|---|---|---|---|---|---|---|---|---|
| **Consumption of Resource** | | | | | | | | |
| Providing an actuarial consultancy service | –264 | 288 | –131 | 969 | 616 | *212* | 679 | 679 |
| **Total Government Actuary's Department Resource Budget** | **–264** | **288** | **–131** | **969** | **616** | ***212*** | **679** | **679** |
| Of which: | | | | | | | | |
| Resource DEL[1] | –264 | 288 | –131 | 969 | 616 | *212* | 679 | 679 |
| **Capital Spending** | | | | | | | | |
| Providing an actuarial consultancy service | 203 | 220 | 193 | 1,515 | 366 | *438* | 238 | 238 |
| **Total Government Actuary's Department Capital Budget** | **203** | **220** | **193** | **1,515** | **366** | ***438*** | **238** | **238** |
| Of which: | | | | | | | | |
| Capital DEL[1] | 203 | 220 | 193 | 1,515 | 366 | *438* | 238 | 238 |
| **Total public spending[2]** | **–183** | **330** | **–53** | **2,217** | **756** | ***228*** | **495** | **495** |

Notes: (1) Department Expenditure Limits set as part of the 2004 Spending Review but realigned to take into account MOG change (Demography work was transferred from GAD to Office for National Statistics in line with the Morris Review recommendations).

(2) Total Public Spending calculated as the total of the resource budget plus the capital budget, less depreciation.

**Table 2: Government Actuary's Department resource budget: voted and non-voted DEL and AME (£000)**

| | 2000-01 Outturn | 2001-02 Outturn | 2002-03 Outturn | 2003-04 Outturn | 2004-05 Outturn | 2005-06 Estimated Outturn | 2006-07 Plans | 2007-08 Plans |
|---|---|---|---|---|---|---|---|---|
| **Providing an actuarial consultancy service** | | | | | | | | |
| **Resource DEL**[(1)] | | | | | | | | |
| **Voted:** | | | | | | | | |
| Request for Resources 1 Administration | –264 | 288 | –131 | 969 | 616 | *212* | 679 | 679 |
| **Total voted** | **–264** | **288** | **–131** | **969** | **616** | ***212*** | **679** | **679** |
| Non voted: | – | – | – | – | – | – | – | – |
| **Total Resource DEL** | –264 | 288 | –131 | 969 | 616 | *212* | 679 | 679 |

NB Voted net resource outturn in Estimate entitled: Government Actuary's Department

| | 2000-01 Outturn | 2001-02 Outturn | 2002-03 Outturn | 2003-04 Outturn | 2004-05 Outturn | 2005-06 Estimated Outturn | 2006-07 Plans | 2007-08 Plans |
|---|---|---|---|---|---|---|---|---|
| **Resource DEL in Estimates**[(2)]**:** | | | | | | | | |
| **Voted:** | | | | | | | | |
| Resource DEL in Budgets | –264 | 288 | –131 | 969 | 616 | *212* | 679 | 679 |
| **Total resource consumption in Estimate** | **–264** | **288** | **–131** | **969** | **616** | ***212*** | **679** | **679** |
| **Total Resource DEL** | –264 | 288 | –131 | 969 | 616 | *212* | 679 | 679 |

Notes:

(1) DEL limits in this table are consistent with definitions used in the 2004 Spending Review but realigned to take into account MOG change (Demography work was transferred from GAD to Office for National Statistics in line with the Morris Review recommendations).

(2) Voted DEL excludes EU receipts included in DEL in Estimates.

**Table 3: Government Actuary's Department capital budget: voted and non-voted DEL (£000)**

| | 2000-01 Outturn | 2001-02 Outturn | 2002-03 Outturn | 2003-04 Outturn | 2004-05 Outturn | 2005-06 Estimated Outturn | 2006-07 Plans | 2007-08 Plans |
|---|---|---|---|---|---|---|---|---|
| **Capital DEL** | | | | | | | | |
| **Voted:** | | | | | | | | |
| Request for Resources 1 Administration | 203 | 220 | 193 | 1,515 | 366[2] | *438* | 238 | 238 |
| **Total voted** | **203** | **220** | **193** | **1,515** | **366** | ***438*** | **238** | **238** |
| Total capital DEL[1] | 203 | 220 | 193 | 1,515 | 366 | *438* | 238 | 238 |
| *of which* | | | | | | | | |
| Voted | 203 | 220 | 193 | 1,515 | 366 | *438* | 238 | 238 |
| *and of which:* | | | | | | | | |
| Central government own spending | 203 | 220 | 193 | 1,515 | 366 | *438* | 238 | 238 |
| NB Voted net capital in Estimates entitled: Government Actuary's Department | | | | | | | | |
| Capital DEL in budgets | 203 | 220 | 193 | 1,515 | 366 | *438* | 238 | 238 |
| **Total net capital in Estimates** | **203** | **220** | **193** | **1,515** | **366** | ***438*** | **238** | **238** |

Notes:
(1) DEL limits in this table are consistent with definitions used in the 2004 Spending Review.
(2) Includes £200K virement from running costs into capital expenditure.

**Table 4: Government Actuary's Department capital employed (£000)**

| | 2000-01 Outturn | 2001-02 Outturn | 2002-03 Outturn | 2003-04 Outturn | 2004-05 Outturn | 2005-06 Estimated Outturn | 2006-07 Plans | 2007-08 Plans |
|---|---|---|---|---|---|---|---|---|
| **Assets on Balance Sheet at start of year** | | | | | | | | |
| Fixed Assets | 339 | 382 | 462 | 1,710 | 1,858 | *2,018* | 1,872 | 1,694 |
| Of which: | | | | | | | | |
| Tangible Assets[1] | 248 | 253 | 247 | 1,571 | 1,541 | *1,640* | 1,550 | 1,451 |
| Intangible Assets[2] | 91 | 129 | 215 | 139 | 317 | *378* | 322 | 243 |
| Current Assets | 3,087 | 2,737 | 3,391 | 3,008 | 2,998 | *3,970* | 3,100 | 3,100 |
| Creditors (<1 year)[4] | 691 | 616 | 1,157 | 1,130 | 986 | *1,610* | 630 | 630 |
| Creditors (>1 year)[3] | 0 | 0 | 0 | 0 | 824 | *1,159* | 1,380 | 1,463 |
| Provisions | 46 | 32 | 27 | 22 | 14 | *9* | 5 | 0 |
| **Capital employed by Government Actuary's Department** | **2,689** | **2,471** | **2,669** | **3,566** | **3,032** | ***3,210*** | **2,957** | **2,701** |

Notes:

(1) Increase in tangible fixed assets represents fit-out costs for Finlaison House and the introduction of a new management information system.

(2) Increase in intangible fixed assets shows the purchase of new software for pensions valuations and electronic records management.

(3) Creditors in 2003-04 and onwards reflect the amounts carried on the accounts to spread over the full term of the lease (20 years) the rent reduction GAD receives for the first five years.

(4) Includes accommodation creditor charged in year

**Table 5: Government Actuary's Department administration budgets (£000)**

| | 2000-01 Outturn | 2001-02 Outturn | 2002-03 Outturn | 2003-04 Outturn | 2004-05 Outturn | 2005-06 Estimated Outturn | 2006-07 Plans | 2007-08 Plans |
|---|---|---|---|---|---|---|---|---|
| **Gross administration costs** | | | | | | | | |
| Paybill | 5,447 | 4,400 | 4,996 | 5,487 | 6,253 | *7,284* | | |
| Other | 1,666 | 1,933 | 1,718 | 2,543 | 3,090 | *3,393* | | |
| **Total gross administration costs** | **7,113** | **6,333** | **6,714** | **8,030** | **9,343** | ***10,677*** | **12,526** | **13,807** |
| Related administration cost receipts | –7,377 | –6,045 | –6,845 | –7,061 | –8,727 | *–10,465* | –11,847 | –13,128 |
| **Total net administration costs** | **–264** | **288** | **–131** | **969** | **616** | ***212*** | **679** | **679** |
| Providing an actuarial consultancy service | –264 | 288 | –131 | 969 | 616 | *212* | 679 | 679 |
| **Total Administration Budget** | **–264** | **288** | **–131** | **969** | **616** | ***212*** | **679** | **679** |

**Table 6: Government Actuary's Department staff numbers**

| | 2000-01 Outturn | 2001-02 Outturn | 2002-03 Outturn | 2003-04 Outturn | 2004-05 Outturn | 2005-06 Estimated Outturn | 2006-07 Plans[1] | 2007-08 Plans[1] |
|---|---|---|---|---|---|---|---|---|
| **Summary** | | | | | | | | |
| Civil Service full time equivalents | 106 | 91.5 | 99.5 | 101 | 106 | 108 | 111 | 114 |
| **By business area** | | | | | | | | |
| Objective 1 | 54 | 56.5 | 66 | 69 | 75 | 78 | 80 | 83 |
| Objective 2 | 29 | 33 | 33.5 | 32 | 31 | 30 | 31 | 31 |
| Objective 3 (moved from GAD in 2001) | 23 | 2 | – | – | – | – | – | – |

Notes:

(1) Our projections for staffing levels in 2006-07 onwards assume that we are able to retain all existing staff whilst continuing with a moderate level of trainees and qualified actuary recruitment.

Printed in the UK by The Stationery Office Limited
on behalf of The Controller of Her Majesty's Stationery Office
187495 05/06 336790 19585